© Gabriel Fleming writemefleming@gmail.com

Dedicated to those
Who have shined their light
And illuminated my darkness

Written in loving memory of
Kaila Mia, Robb Hawes, and Joel Kirby.
I pray that you have found your everlasting light.

Juxtaposition

By Gabriel Fleming

Part One:

Darkness

The Last Butterfly Show

    I stood behind a young couple in line for the last Show of the Butterfly. They were an adorable little couple of future alcoholics, flowing with relentless anticipation of their next poisonous concoction, possessing no fear or thought whatsoever of a hangover, they probably never even experienced one....yet.
    Later on, as the line digressed and the butterfly began to flap its wings, I learned that the young man and I shared the same name, and so far, also the love and hope for his intimate counterpart that I once had, but lost long ago. Something in me wanted to warn this young winged messenger of things to come. So I tapped 'myself' on the shoulder and turned around at the same time.
    "What up?" he said. Fucking young punks.
    "Excuse me," I said. "I couldn't help but overhear that your name is Gabriel?"
    "Yeah, so?" Fucking young punks.
    "So, mine is, too," I said calmly.
    His girl, or at least the girl who was with him, whatever, upon my saying that my name is the same as the guy she was with, made her eyes sparkle like diamonds; she moaned a little subtle, "Oh." As if she had found a better Gabriel, and wanted to use my arm as a mantle for her trophy ass. But I brushed her off; I thought to myself, "Step aside, jailbait."

What I said next was what I thought a potentially better version of me needed to hear.

"Gabriel, from one to another, slow down. Don't blow your horns too soon and knock the wrong walls down. The world can wait, and believe me, for you it surely will. Write about this day, and every one that follows." He sort of shrugged it off, but I think he got the message.

I started to turn away, but quickly turned back to face him, for I had forgot the best advice that I could have given to myself.

"Gabriel," I said.

"Yeah?"

"One more thing," I started saying to him, but looking at her. I grabbed her and kissed her, right in front of him. I pulled her in close for personal closure; I kissed her long and hard, as I once used to do.

Once I was done I released her and said to him, "Don't make her cry anymore. She will leave you."

Then I got on the wings of the butterfly, and took my last flight.

Poison

Chemical trails are in my sight

Pulsating like heartbeats in my eyes

A metronome of love

From the clipped wings of a dove

Read these poetic lines

I swear to God I'm fine

Read between the lines

The fine print proves I'm lying

I yearn for human contact

But I love to be alone

This hard truth

Makes me desire to atone

When you abandoned me and my lonesome soul

Nothing else could fill that hole

I couldn't seem to give a fuck

I never was a man of good luck

I could say I miss the Devils brew

A whole lot more than I miss you

You still haunt me in my dreams

When I lay me down to sleep

So I became an insomniac

I can never find relief

Choices

I looked up 'isolation' in my own thesaurus

And it read 'contentment'

I looked up 'exclusion' in my own thesaurus

And it read 'loneliness'

If you let me be alone

I will be glad

If you leave me alone

I'll probably be sad

You will have to make the decision for me

Either leave me alone

Or just let me be

Otherwise I'll choose to be with you

But I don't have a word for that

Voodoo

Your twisted heart still hangs on my wall

I pierced it with a pin

I often take it down

Just to hold it

I feel it beating

I feel it beating the life out of itself

I put it back on the wall

After I pierce it again and again

Every time I take it down

There is a new hole

I hold it for a long time

Squeezing it

Choking you

Still beating

Just to put another pin in it

There are now many holes

I wonder if you can feel them

Your twisted heart is still beating

Tennessee Whiskey From Ireland

I have a furrowed brow

I don't know why or how

I think I'm depressed

Does that make you impressed?

What do I do now?

I carry not a smile but a frown

I can't tell what's got me so down

I do what I can

But I don't have a plan

They call me The Partyless Clown

My hands are balled up in fists

So tight that there's veins on my wrists

I don't have a clue

What I'm going to do

I'm at the end of my wits

The thoughts in my head are racing

My leg is constantly shaking

I'm feeling a bit queasy

They said this would be easy

But back and forth I'm still pacing

The insides of my palms are sweaty

The weight on my heart is heavy

My thoughts are too deep

That it's hard for me to sleep

Wide awake for my demons I'm ready

Confusion

My hair is completely different

My voice is completely different

My clothes are completely different

My thoughts are completely different

My opinions are completely different

My laugh is completely different

My friends are completely different

My heart is completely different

But my face is exactly the same

Yet I do not recognize it

Nor do I like what I see

Entrance/Exit

"Someone's at the door"

I often heard her scream

There was never anyone there

"Someone's at the door," she screamed

"No there's not," I replied

Though this time she was right

It burst through the house

With a fierce magnetic force

Taking its grip on me

"Someone's out the door," I screamed

Now she constantly stands in the door frame

Waiting for that someone to be at the door

Transfusion

I can feel the hot blood

Rushing up my body

It melts my bones

It's boiling

I could probably swallow an egg and shit it out edible

Well, maybe after you wash it

It begins at my toes

It moves up my legs

It feels like I'm stepping into a hot spring

The blood reaches my cock

I'm used to that one

It moves up my chest

Makes my heart beat fast

Going down my arms now

Feels like heroin

It tingles my fingers

Balls up my fists

But I'm too tired of fighting

Now it reaches my head

Will I explode?

If I do, will anyone even miss m—

KABOOM!!

Run Away On A Runway

I look at the birds with envy

They fly through the sky

With such ease

All they do is flap their wings

And reach the clouds

It seems as though they do not tire

I am jealous of the birds

Not because they can fly

But because they are not

Exhausted by the process

Religion Falters At The Altar

Where is this God?

Where is this God when the mass ends?

Where is this God when the masses win?

Where is he when mothers cry,

When fathers flee and brothers die?

Where is he when a child is touched by a priest

Watched over by the Lords last feast?

Where is he during times of war,

When hate is stitched, but love is tore?

Where is this God in a nation of poverty?

That starving child asks,

"Why does he care for you, but has abandoned me?"

Where is this God when a mother is beat,

In front of her son,

Raised to think that is the way to be?

Why does he answer your prayers?

Then rejects those of the needy; it's not fair.

I ask you again,

But you don't know.

Where is this God?

Will he ever show?

Doing The Same Thing, Fuck The Results

Being insane seemed insane

Am I crazy or am I plain?

What a wonderful game

It's hard to decipher the difference

To harmonize the two makes more sense

My thoughts are capsizing

My mind is getting dense

My heart is a little more heavy

Am I prepared?

Am I ready?

I think and I think and I think

And I drink and I drink and I drink

In these shallow waters, I will never sink

For my insides are hollow

Even my demons they follow

My sweet chariot swings low

Am I crazy or am I plain?

What a wonderful game

Don't Make Me Beg

Dear God

Above me

Beside me

All around me

We don't talk much anymore

But I pray of you now

As I lean on bended knee

The center piece

In a puddle

Lake

River

Now a sea

Of blood

I say now, O God

I pray of you, O Lord

To also take me

Junk

The heat then hits you

As if you were facing a fire

Then you feel weightless

Yet heavy

As if you were a feather

Floating down

Gaining speed

By the anchor attached

You itch

Doesn't make a difference

It feels so good to scratch

You're induced with a cool, darkened horizon

You slip in and out

Of a dream within a dream

You haven't a care in the world

Not even the fact that you're a feather

Attached to an anchor

You enjoy falling

For at least you're still flying

I-Rock

I am a suicide bomber

Wearing a bright red jacket

I blend in really well

Yet everyone notices me

It's only after the explosion

When I am described for what I wore

"The man in the bright red jacket"

Will people then recognize me

They'll say, "Hey, I saw that man in a coffeeshop!

Before the explosion

I noticed his jacket

But I didn't notice his face."

It seems that what we do in life

Bears little resemblance in valor

When compared to how we die.

Happy Holidays Ya Filthy Animal

I like New Year's Eve

I get to dress fancy

Then get drunk

I like St. Patty's Day

I get to wear my favorite color

Then get drunk

And Halloween, of course

I can finally be someone else

Then get drunk

I like all holidays

Because I get drunk

But it's only on Valentine's Day

When I also get dressed up and get drunk

But I get to wear my ex's skin

Pocket The Cards, Bitch

I must have been miles away

When I finally heard the sound

I took the first step towards it

Then a second

It drew me closer

And closer

I took a left

Then a right

Turned around

For the sound started fading

Took another left

And continued walking

With the sound getting louder

And louder

As I got closer

Closer

I started running

My pace quickened

As the volume increased

Then I was facing it

I reluctantly walked inside

And there I was

With the two of you

And your sounds of spiteful pleasure

I heard it

But more so felt it

Pulsate in my broken heart

Flooded

I screamed out your name

Followed by a whispered "I love you"

All I got back was silence

Spoken through your fear bearing eyes

My devastation took it's course

And kicked the remaining feelings right out the door

I locked myself in my solemn prison

That I built inside my head

There was no more of you

Just my drugs instead

I cried, but it didn't show

"My God, what have you done to me?"

Why there were no tears I do not know

There was no one who could answer my plea

I relentlessly continued

"My God, how can this be?"

One day she'll see

Her animosity

Her brutality

And the absurdity

It all occurred

On our anniversary

How desperate I am

For a remedy to cure my sickness

But the cause of it all

Just always seemed to fit best

I can't help but to wonder why

The ocean shelters the sky

Why the animals are all shy

Why the moon is so high

And why you had to say goodbye

A man stuck in the rain

Told me there's no reason to complain

No reason to live in vain

That no one has ever died from standing in the rain

But how could he comprehend my pain

His words mean nothing

But scorn and disdain

He's not aware

That my heart has been slain

Everything you have done

Will always remain

I Rode Through The Desert On A Dame With No Name

How can I tell the difference

Between the truth and a lie

When all of your faces are the same?

I've lost all feelings for you

You're just another dame

I love you

But I hate you

Yes, I hate you

But I just can't seem to stay away

All that I long for

Is honesty and truth

An end to your hypocrisy

Another year of youth

A different way of seeing things

And a different version of you

Animosity overwhelms me

As I hungrily seek sweet sentiments

A concrete peek into our fate

Unfortunately for you, my dear

All I feel is hate

If you have nothing nice to say

Then just keep your sweet lips shut

You've ruined my life

And enough is enough

How am I to tell the difference

Between a friend and a lover

If you were still with him

While we were together?

In his eyes I wasn't good enough for you

I begged for forgiveness in the cold weather

I hope you have a wonderful life with him

I'll stand in the shadows

Continue to dim

Your lack of reply no longer affects me

When you come back around I'll be gone

I've made a shit ton of mistakes, dear

But the biggest one of them all was you

I love you

But I hate you

Yes, I hate you

But I just can't seem to stay away

Part Two:

Illumination

Dead End

Everyone will walk a road

Everyone will reach that blind man's crossroad

Everyone will have to make a choice of direction

Just to continue walking some more

Why do you have to choose?

You don't know your destination

You've walked far enough

You're tired

Just lie down

And sleepwalk

Cliffhanger

How close can you get

To the edge of a cliff

Without falling over?

What if you never leave the edge?

Climbing down it

Enduring all of the obstacles

On the way down to safety

Touch ground

Blow Her

She was like Jazz

Hell

She was Jazz

Her glance struck chords in your heart

Her touch instructed the butterflies to dance

Her voice teased your ears

As if you were truly listening for the first time

Her body made you want to ask her for a dance

Her smell stuck with you

Like a song stuck in your head

Her laugh harmonized like the trumpets of the angels

Her walk made people dance

An unorganized rhythm to move out of her way

And her kiss

God, her kiss makes you want to sing

For an instrumental band

She was just Jazz

Bee On A Bicycle

I shuffled the deck

She dealt out the hands

"Do you have any threes?" she asked.

Go fish

"Do you have any kings?"

She gave them to me

"Do you have any regrets about us?"

No answer

"Do you have any fives?"

Go fish

"Do you have any twos?"

I gave them to her

"Do you have any drugs in your system?"

Go fish

I was bluffing

"Do you have any jacks?"

She gave them to me

"Are you still seeing him?"

Go fish

"Do you still love me?"

Go fish

I smiled

She rolled her eyes and asked for an ace

Go fish

"Do you still love me?"

She smiled, "Go fish."

I grabbed her and kissed her

Her cards fell to the ground

I won

Raindrop

I can't explain the meaning of life

I can't explain a parent's severity in their strife

I can't explain the definition of love

I sure can't tell you if there's a Heaven above

I can't tell you what we're doing here

These answers will never be clear

I can't explain anything at all

Only how the rain falls

Your eyes mimic your heart

I fear the day that we part

Listen to the rainfall

I think we are

What we should not be

Please explain to me where we stand

You said we are somewhere

But we are nowhere

Alone together

Forever and ever

Two lovers in the nightfall

Just listening to the rainfall

Astronomy

As long as you were wrapped around me here

I was a man without fear

I never shed a single tear

I'll always love you

This much is clear

We're still close

No matter how far

We'll make more of the most

This sure ain't romance from a bar

This is, for every person, a star

I can't help but to hum along

When you whispered in my ear

That sweet and sultry song

We'll be together

Until the day I'm gone

Unless you let me

Take you along

You had me right from the start

I'll gladly relinquish whatever's left of my heart

This thing we have is a work of art

A masterpiece complete

Not one missing part

I can see the light of day

There are no words that I can say

No games in which we play

I'll be in love with you

Forever and a day

You're the one I choose to call my dear

Listen up and I'll tell you what you need to hear

I'll always hold you near

Just stay wrapped around me here

New connections

I'm alive again

I'm finally free

I'd be a liar to say that no one

Forewarned me

That this life

Would cost a small fee

This is the life I live

My purpose is defined

By the love that I give

No longer do I ask myself, "What if"

For I now know

This is the life I am to live

My father once said

"The first year's a bitch"

But it can't be worse

Than when I was left for dead in a ditch

My past consumes me

From there to here

But I no longer

Have to live in fear

For this is the life I am to live

This is the life I live

Listen to the advice that I give

Life every single day

As if it were your last

Live for today

Fuck what's in the past

The life that you live

Will be the life that I love

For this is the life I know we are to live

Hello

This is the last time

I'll look into your eyes

To win back your love

I've tried and retried

This is the last time

I'll see your face

Bending over backwards

Just for one last embrace

This is the last time

To say the final goodbyes

Your incomparable smile

Your sweet mysterious eyes

Reminds me of a time

When butterflies

And subway cars

Lined our lives

I can't take another minute of this pain

So long, my dear

I'll catch the next train

Aroused by winter chills

And your hand made scarves

We get our thrills

Punctuated by the thought of the first move

These memories I will never lose

I know when to say goodbye

Yet we can never deny

Our stranded and remaining love

For it will be a lie

Drunken confessions

Revealed over the phone

Remind me of the fact

That I will always have a home

This is the last time

That I will hold your hand

Your many faces

Your infinite spaces

I'll never understand

Just know

Whatever happens, my dear

That I will always be right behind you

In case you fall

I'll forever be here

Valentine's Day

It was December when I met you

In the chill of a wintry night

I glanced at you

Saw that you were glancing too

I said I never met anyone

As radiant as you

And all you did was wonder

If I was telling the truth

A couple days went past

I convinced you

To cut ties with him

Gave you the key to my world

Told you that at anytime

You were welcome to come in

You said you never felt

These feelings this fast

And that you were scared

About whether or not it would last

I said, "Don't you worry, babe

Everything will be okay

As long as you stick by me

Day after day."

Then Valentine's Day came and went

And you gave me a poorly written book

About all the times that we spent

I took off my jacket

Gave it to you

You said that you didn't

Want this day to ever be through

And it was on the ride back home

When there was something in the air

That made you whisper

"I'm in love with you, I swear."

You made me feel again

As I flew with the doves

And I'll always remember

The 14th Day Of Love

Chamomile Tea

The city buses

Swept through the avenues

My eyes are getting tired

And all my money's spent

I wouldn't have it any other way

I'm going back to where I belong

To be happy, joyous, and free

With a mindset of complete serenity

Mr. Sandman, won't you deliver me

The happiest of my melancholy dreams

I live a chaotic lifestyle

This much is very true

I'm always running around

And my mind is running too

Those stinking flowers

Will have to wait

There's way too much

Shit on my plate

I wouldn't have it any other way

I'm just another mere human

In this beautiful mess of a world

Another pawn on a checker pattern board

Watching the strategy unfurl

We are just tokens

To be played in the game of life

Struggling to deal

With our day in, day out strife

I wouldn't have it any other way

Now it is time

To lay down your head

And release all of today's

Trash you've been fed

The tension in your life

Is going away

Along with your stiff neck

Until the next day

I wouldn't have it any other way

Rule Breaker

Our love has passed away

Yet the feeling still remains

Behind the dark and foggy

Sunglass frames

Every time I see you

My heart starts beating fast

And my heart rate increases

Faster than the last

They tell me to treat everyone

As if I were in their shoes

That bullshit hypocrisy

They call The Golden Rule

But then they will say

"Rules are meant to be broken"

And that is the case with you

For you tied me up

Imprisoned me from the world

And you kept me from

What I needed to see

Then you released me

From my small cramped cage

With my newfound freedom

Lifted too was my rage

Yet I still carry around

My dark empty cage

Now everything I do

Reminds me of you

I guess the feeling still remains

Dizzy

She turned and she twirled

Like a merry go round

Beneath the hypnotic sunset

A better time

I could not have found

Let go and let me

Take you down

We'll paint the seductive color

All over this town

Back and forth

Like a merry go round

You woke up bare

In the tranquil moonlight

In the windowsill

Your body radiated the color of love

And I imagined

That this must be Heaven

As I listened to the sweet sound

Of peaceful sounding doves

I revealed in a whisper

That what I searched for I found

And we dreamt of our future together

On the merry go round

And we didn't mind

What everyone thought

For we knew the web of truth

In which we were caught

To them we were really

Just something they were not

To halves that made a whole

And our blood was running hot

They were just blind people

No ability to see

That love would be on our side

Eternally

Two young kids

Whose love knew no bounds

Forever riding

On our merry go round

Sweet Cakes

She had purple hair

It was interesting

A radiant face

Symmetrical, with perfect features

She said she had shingles

But she was far too young

And with her hair the color that it was

I asked, "Other than that, Mrs. Kennedy

How was the parade?"

She didn't look amused

For when the magic bullet hit

She heard someone say,

"He wasn't nothing but a nigger lover anyway"

She had a laugh

That could shake the earth

And wore a statement chain

Around her chest

Halfway completing

My duties of domination

She had on Guess jeans

But her ass had all the answers

Her name was Debbie

But there was nothing little about her

And I would gladly eat her all up

Beams of Light

Your warmth covers me

Like the linens in our bed

And it fills my face

Like the blood rushing

When you make me blush

The brightness of your smile blinds me

I'm cautioned not to gaze

You help me to grow

Like the flowers so beautiful

You help me stay straight

Like the planets' alignment in space

You are my sunshine

I revolve around you

Hiking On Cement

I love the sound of a burning cigarette

Like the crackle of fallen leaves

I love the sound of sirens

Like the wolves of the woods

I love the height of the buildings

Like that of an aging oak tree

I love the sound of the cars zooming past

Like the stampede of fleeing deer

I love the howl of peoples laughter

Like the rain amongst the trees

I love the blinding light of a neon sign

Like early sunlight through a naked branch

I love my urban jungle

The electric forest that is my city

Surrender To Win

    I was stuck in my thoughts alone. I marched towards a required hour of battle, a battle that would guarantee freedom from an enemy disguised as an ally. My fellow comrades marched alongside me, though they seemed braver than I, for to suffer through a hell like I had endured, the battle for infinite freedom seemed as though it would be the hardest to be fought.
    I noticed then that my fellow men were unarmed. Certain foolishness, I thought! I clung tightly to my thoughts familiar, for they were my armor, and impenetrable at that; my fists with knuckles white, prepared to fight and express those old familiar mental bullets whilst in this harsh combat. Tight those fists were, until an illuminated lightning bug landed upon them.
    "To surrender is to win," it told me, shining brighter than before.
    "Buzz off," I sarcastically replied, shaking my fists to knock him off.
    "Trust me," he said, clinging on for his life. "My ass is on fire, too. But look at your comrades."
    I looked, and I still saw bold souls with no weapons. Then I realized.

"Ah, no weapons, they have surrendered," I proclaimed. "Yet how will they win the battle with no weapons?"

"They let go of their old familiar ways of thinking, and armed themselves with the thoughts of those who have won," he stated as we approached the building.

He continued, "Use those pages that were granted to you as a field guide, then, and only then, will the battle become easier."

I persistently inquired, "But tell me how a book will protect me in this enemy territory?"

"You blind fool! That isn't enemy territory. Hell, it's practically your headquarters!"

We approached the so called 'headquarters', and our time was cut short, yet the little bug still stayed on my finger.

"Mr. Firefly, with your infinite wisdom, why do you stay on my hand?" I asked.

"You are bigger than I am," he answered. "That is a long way down if my own wings were to fail me, therefore it will take a power greater than myself such as you to help me touch ground."

"Fair enough," I said as I placed him upon a leaf. "Though I hardly consider myself to be a higher power than yourself, what with the wisdom you have granted me."

He looked up at me from his leaf and said, "We help each other out, that's how it works. Run along now, your freedom awaits. I will be here when you come out."

I walked through the door, unarmed and surrendered, yet stronger than ever because of it.

Part Three

Notes of a Dirty Young Man

"You were right to create such an accurate and sensible euphemism for the trials and tribulations I've endured throughout my life; I am indeed a novel that is difficult to read for emotional reasons, but you just can't seem to lose your place. Keep turning those pages, love."

"Charming," she said. "I feel I should express a level of pleasure for helping you acknowledge a deep rooted part of who you truly are, but first I must ask a question."

Taking a drag of his cigarette, and speaking through exhaled smoke, "Shoot," he said.

"Why do you tell me all of these things?" she asked. "Like, what makes me so special? You would think that we were communicating through a screened divider, and I was sport a white collar similar to a Hitler stache."

She finally made him smile, chuckle at that. Then more sincerely he replied, "It's hard to tell, really. I'm generally pretty upfront about my experiences to anyone who would hear them; I guess it's on the off chance that they will take it upon themselves to write what I never had the courage to."

He finally made her frown, cry at that.

It's nice to have someone to talk to, someone who you could share mutual interests with, highlights of our work week, but most importantly, the lowlights of our mind. That's the sweet stuff, the shit you wouldn't dare let other people know, only them.

We weren't bad people trying to be good, we were sick people trying to get well. We often thought to ourselves, were we alone together, or were we together alone?
A love never had is still a love lost. We met each other in the restaurant that we were both employed at. I was a bartender, and she was a pastry chef. And after each shift, I would go back to her place and, in so many words, she drank my cocktails, and I ate her cookies, so to speak.
It didn't last long though. She didn't like how much I drank, regardless of the fact that whenever she got drunk, she would drink herself into a blackout. I also now notice that I only 'ate her cookies' when we were drunk. It was essentially premeditated. And as the drinks poured, so did our hearts, until we got to the bottom of the bottle, where the glass became clear, along with our intentions.
When we sobered up the next day and went to work, we hardly initiated any contact, aside from the not so subtle flirtatious glances. It was as if we became connected to quickly, then disconnected too suddenly.

I often notice myself staring into a blank space, an infinite nothing. But it is in this nothingness that I comprehend everything. Shit, I have to be in space to realize I'm all there. Now they tell me I've lost my mind, but really, I've never felt closer to it.

When I die, won't you cut out your heart and bury my with it? You never use it and it's mine anyway. I'll need something to keep me warm. On second thought, being that I'm going to hell, I'd probably just eat it. I hear a bitch's heart is packed with nutrition.

She was beautiful when she spoke. She had a sincere tone about ideals universal. Her eyes shined bright like stars, carrying me off to a mystical place afar. She was a celestial guide to the knowledge unknown.

I was smart, but not wise. I had a shit ton of knowledge, but lacked common sense. Life is a test I did not study for. I think a lot more brilliantly than I speak.

I have sick thoughts. The same ones that everyone has but doesn't talk about, like wanting to fuck your kid's babysitter or dropping a penny off the Empire State Building. The only thing that separates me from the rest of society is that I would probably turn those thoughts into actions; fuck it, I'll even throw a quarter.

When I finally got out of bed after three days of detoxing and walked outside, I could have sworn that I was seeing the world for the very first time. Everything was so bright and everyone that I saw had big smiles on their faces. What the fuck do they have to be so goddamn happy about? I discovered right then that they all had something, be it a baby, a dog, or a significant other. I never felt so alone, and I no longer wanted to live.

She told me to hit her while we were fucking. I'll be honest with you, I was uncomfortable at first. I was afraid that I would hurt her. I told her so and she told me that that was the whole point of it, and that I should 'stop being a pussy and hit her for Christ's sakes'. I eased into it at first and before I knew it her face was red and her cunt was wet. I ended up enjoying it a little too much, to the point where I would strike her outside of the bedroom, when I thought she deserved it. It always led to passionate fucking afterwards, until one day she left my apartment with a black eye and never returned.

Now, because of that, I have a discussion with the women who I'm about to fuck, asking whether or not they like it rough and to what extent.

"Hey, stud," she said. "You got a light?"

"For you? Anything." I held the flame in front of her already glowing face. She took a drag and began coughing violently. "First time smoking?" I asked.

"No," she laughed. "I'm sick."

"Hey, me too."

"Physically?"

"No, mentally."

"So is everyone else," she said. "But I have a cold."

"Gee," I said. "I wish I had a cold."

"I can give it to you if you really want it that bad," she said behind a smirk. Then she gave me her cold, twice that night, then once again the next morning.

She had wavy hair that came down to her shoulders, and looked wet, like she just touched shore after swimming in the ocean. Her eyes were the same color as that very same sea, and were sure as hell the same size. Her smile looked like the reflection of the moon on the calm steady waves. She threw me a lifeline, but I chose instead to drown in her.

I decided to write from then on; only I didn't know how to do right, I've always done wrong.

They toasted to their mutual desires, to have someone who truly appreciates being in their life, and who cherishes their presence. To tie the toast, he clinked his beer can to her glass of sweet tea. They were both coming out of very eccentric, yet tiring relationships. They reconnected at the best time, and the worst time, with respects to Chuck Dickhead.

There was something strange about their midnight encounters; one night would be filled with passion and joy, and the following night could be filled with the most awkward form of sexual tension. Part of him thought that it had to be because of their past relationships, and the accompanied fear that the outcome of those loves once past would transfer over to what they were building, regardless of any tensions. They were afraid that they would ruin everything.

Then again, his mind would begin to race around in circles with the idea that he was the only person who felt this way, and that really she was just enjoying the time that they were spending together. He would begin to drift away, standing only a few inches away from her all the while.

It was merely his defects getting the best of him. If he found someone that he could freely be himself around, he would need to have a more concrete definition of what the relationship actually was. He thought with his heart, and he felt with his brain.

I used to find joy in unhappy things. The things that made me sad, after realizing them, at least made me feel alive, and I used that as a means to carry on. The funny thing is though, after I ended things with her, I realized that she was the only thing that made me feel so unhappy. I always felt judged by her, she didn't appreciate the person I was. Here I am clinging on to unhappy feelings, when the source of it all was the person that I was spending the most time with. I had to let go.

I was writing in my notebook, nothing too special, just a short story about those surrounding me. Anyway, I saw a man drawing beautiful portraits, of those surrounding us.

"How can you capture everyones face and draw them so flawlessly?" I asked him.

"How can you write about them so flawlessly?" he replied. "Your pen and my brush move as the same constant pace as their lives, and our minds."

They should offer a 'Paranoid Package' at hospitals, consisting of full skeletal, physical, STD and blood exams, with a free psychiatric examination.

She was my type completely. Everything about her was; everything from her fire red hair, full pouty lips of the same color, along with the beautifully structured art exhibit that was her body, which I carefully analyzed, glancing twice over at each and ever colorful piece, pondering to myself the question of what god was thinking about when he created this one. Plus, she was a barista so I knew she could keep me up all night.

I am very fucked up right now. A not so hidden addiction camouflaged by a falsified appearance of self control. The thoughts that drift through my mind present the bittersweet consequence of altering said mind. At the same time, my mood would be the centerpiece of it all. If I'm in a joyous mood when I'm intoxicated, then I would either think of the moment that I am in, or I would reminisce of memories. But if I am feeling anxious, sad, or angry, I would almost always have obsessive thoughts about a past lover; normally bad memories, but a good one would sneak in every so often. It keeps me up at night.

Then again, maybe I'm just making excuses to reach oblivion. One will never fully know.

"I need for a real man to fuck me," she blatantly said. "Nothing else could get me off better."

"You don't say," I said.

"Are you a real man?"

She put me on the spot. It was a loaded question; of course any man would consider himself a 'real man', it's that or Pinocchio. Though I hardly feel manly lately. She set me on fire two completely opposite ways. It was sensual, and hostile. I couldn't tell if she was just busting my balls, or if she was actually curious as to whether or not I could keep up the pace in her bed. She was still looking at me, waiting for an answer. My dumb smirk wasn't answering for me, so I took a gulp of beer, lit a cigarette, gulped without beer, and answered her.

"Well," I said. "I'd like to think so." Idiot.

"That's not good enough," she said. I knew it wouldn't be. "I'd rather have someone who knows for a fact that they're a man."

I smirked again, this time looking directly at her, then suddenly I hit puberty.

"Look," I said. "I don't know who you think you are, but I know who I am. And I know that I was man enough to answer your question. Whether or not *you* can keep up with *me* in bed, well, you'll just have find that out."

"Okay, man, let's go."

Stella By Starlight

'You never forget your first love' is the most truthful cliché there is. However, I think it would be more truthful if the 'forget' is replaced with 'get over'. Forgetting is one thing, but it's easier. In order to forget someone, you have to get over them, and that's nearly impossible, unless you have assistance from a substitute lover that eventually turns into a replacement partner; or if your first love caused you so much deliberate pain, in any sense of the word, that the thought of doing it all over again with someone knew sounds exhausting. In the latter situation, it winds up being the person that caused you the most pain the worst form of karma, along with an accompanying dependency to it, while you move on just as naturally as you feel pain.

This is my destined scenario. I will never fall out of love with her. But I fucked up with a capital *F*. I started getting high again, and she became replaced by my vices. I was also in art school at the time, had my first apartment, both of which I lost. I should have known that it would happen, I should have known when I lost her. When I moved back in with my parents, I went back to her. I should have known things would only get worse. I should have known a lot of things.

I tried to get clean again, and I used her for support. I actually managed to get quite some time under my belt, it took the same amount of time to convince her to be with again. I kept saying that I 'changed', and I made her fall in love with me again, even harder than the first time, if that was even possible. None of it lasted very long. The breakup this time was easier, still difficult because it was still a breakup, but it was easier to absorb. We were both an emotional wreck, and we knew that our relationship wasn't helping. We began to grow apart.

However, we graciously agreed to still have sex, which somewhat led to the third encounter. Not before I had another breakdown, naturally. It took her so long to see me again. I really can't recall exactly how it happened, but after one of my thousand attempts to reach out and see her, she finally agreed to one. It was so excellent. We went to our favorite diner, where my parents used to meet when they started dating, actually, and talked like we never left each other.

Then one night, she was having problems at her mother's house, so I took it upon myself to invite her to spend the night at my place, and we kissed. That's all, just one kiss, but God was it a kiss, fireworks and shit. It was at this time in our drawn out relationship, where I felt that betraying her was pointless, I finally understood that, so I respected her more. She will deny this until the sun goes dark, but it really is the truth. We really only ever had each other. Naturally we started sleeping with each other again, but she put a stop to that real quick.

In between the second and third encounters, I signed up for one of those evil dating apps, her friend had one, too. I admit that at first the app was used to get me some easy tail, but it eventually got old, so I started using it to find characters for my stories. She unfortunately found the whole thing interesting and eventually set up an account herself.

This, in my opinion, was the beginning of where we stand now. She claimed that she was just using it for fun. Then all of a sudden, she seemed to have dropped off the face of the earth. I knew exactly what happened, because she led me on so strongly at first, then within weeks of her downloading that fucking app she vocally assured me that there wouldn't be another romantic connection between us, but that the app was for 'entertainment purposes only'. Yeah, and the sky is fucking blue; oh, wait. Anyway, I tried to reach out to her several times, but got the dial tone every single time.

We finally caught up with each other and it was on that day that I found out that she was seeing someone else. I felt betrayed; I felt how I'm sure she felt every time I hurt her, (our levels of emotion are very different). We tried to remain friends, but like the good alcoholic that I was I went on a drunken rant about once a week, filling my empty bottles with tears until she hung up on me. One of the main things that pissed me off so much was that the guy and I were so similar, we even had the same fucking birthday. Fortunately for me, they didn't last long. To my satisfaction, she even gossiped to me about the fact that he was a shitty lay with a small dick, but she could have been faking that fact to make me feel better, I hear women do that sometimes. She ended things with him in the harshest way possible, and apparently the only way that she knew how to, by just hanging him up to dry. I loved that.

  We started having regular outings and even more regular sex again. But things ended for the final time just because of our difference of opinion. We had both changed so much, in the way we viewed everything, even each other. She became a feminist and me, well let's just say I love women in a different way. But more importantly, we had become so accustomed to the pain that we caused each other that we forgot how to make each other happy. We just knew that we didn't want to be alone, and that we were each other's fail safe, but we called it off regardless.

  No matter what, I could never get over her. Even when I claim to hate her, I still feel so protective over her; which is probably a big part of why I accepted that she and I couldn't be together, I couldn't hurt her anymore. It was hurting me, too; I get consumed with mental chaos over her, whether she is in or out of my life. Yet, I know that right now I could probably hold together a relationship with her again, but it isn't worth the risk, for I do not know what tomorrow brings.

In fact, when I hand wrote this chronicle of love proclamation, my pen ran out of ink. She caused my pen to run out of ink, my tongue to run out of blood, my mind to run out of poison, and my heart to run out of an antidote, all hidden within my empty pen.

If you are reading this, just know that I still love you, I always have, and I always will.

Special thanks to my parents, my friends and family, all of the women, and with honorable mentions to Jay Shoemake, Ella Alexander, Amanda Carroll, Robert Hartle, Meredith Jones, Kenji Shoeboot, Caitlin Lochridge, Adam LaBorde, Royia Rozati, Randy Dalton, and all of the New Connections I have made. Your presence lies within these pages.